· LOCAL · FLAVOUR · SERIES ·

COOKING
&
LOOKING
in
CANBERRA

Compiled and
illustrated by

· Rosemary ·
· Sinclair ·

Edited by

· Joy ·
· Hayes ·

AYERS & JAMES HERITAGE BOOKS
Sydney 1986

© Rosemary Sinclair, 1986
Illustrated by Rosemary Sinclair
Designed by Judy Hungerford
Project editing by Joy Hayes, Creative Pages
Project management by Book Production Services Pty Ltd
Typeset and assembled by Rochester Photosetting Service
Printed in Singapore
ISBN 0 949256 02 1

* C·O·N·T·E·N·T·S *

ON MEASUREMENTS

Trying new recipes has long been one of my favourite pastimes, and because the major difficulty encountered has been working out stipulated measurements, I've tried to make the recipes easy for everybody to follow.

Keeping in mind that cooking is an art, *not* a science, I've used cup measurements where practicable (i.e. ordinary tea-cup size not the little dainty one!). Otherwise, measurements are given in both the metric and imperial scales.

Some cooks believe it necessary to weigh everything, but I've never done so, and can't recall any failures as a result.

GENERAL MEASUREMENTS
FOR SCALE-SCORNING COOKS

1 breakfast cup sieved flour, lightly filled	125 g	= 4 oz
1 breakfast cup liquid	250 ml	= ½ pt
2 breakfast cups solid butter	500 g	= 1 lb
2 breakfast cups granulated sugar	500 g	= 1 lb
2½ breakfast cups icing sugar	500 g	= 1 lb
1 tablespoon butter, rounded	60 g	= 2 oz
2 tablespoons flour, rounded	30 g	= 1 oz
2 tablespoons desiccated coconut (level)	30 g	= 1 oz
2 dessertspoons liquid (1 tablespoon)	20 ml	
2 teaspoons (1 dessertspoon)	10 ml	
4 teaspoons (1 tablespoon)	20 ml	
1 teaspoon	5 ml	

Note: North American readers need to remember that their tablespoon equals 15 ml or 3 teaspoons.

OVEN TEMPERATURES

It is difficult to advise exact oven temperatures as different makes of stoves give different results at the same temperature reading. Indeed, many fuel stoves still in use have no temperature gauge, and a degree of guesswork is unavoidable.

The following chart should be helpful for most stoves.

OVEN DESCRIPTION	TEMPERATURE GAUGE		
	Automatic Electric	*Gas*	*0°C (or Celsius)*
Cool	200	200	100
Very slow	250	250	120
Slow	300–325	300	150–160
Moderately slow	325–350	325	160–170
Moderate	350–375	350	170–190
Moderately hot	375–400	375	190–200
Hot	400–450	400	200–230
Very hot	450–500	450	230–260

Black Mt. Tower
across the Lake from
Weston Park.

* I·N·T·R·O·D·U·C·T·I·O·N *

The character of a city is largely determined by the people who live there. Canberra, Australia's national capital, has two distinct groups of residents, and it is their interaction which makes it a unique city.

The first group are the city's permanent residents. Among them are workers transferred from other parts of the country, and descendants of Canberra's pioneers who struggled to settle in an inhospitable environment. They lived there long before the city was proclaimed the nation's capital and remain rightfully proud of their heritage.

The second group includes those in diplomatic missions and government departments, parliamentarians, parliamentary staff and journalists representing Australia-wide media. Most are transients and while some are given to criticisms of Canberra as a 'soulless city', they rarely look too far behind the city's ordered facade.

Canberra, by any standards, is one of the world's most attractive cities, although it was not until 1963 that the Molonglo River was dammed to create Lake Burley Griffin, around which the designer's city is planned. People and houses seem to be outnumbered by the trees that enhance the city with seasonal beauty. While Canberra boasts an ever-increasing number of modern shopping complexes, the corner store character still exists with shopping centres serving every suburb. It is a city whose fortunate residents can measure travel time by distance rather than non-negotiable traffic. It is a growing city with a population in 1985 of more than a quarter of a million. It will always be one of my favourite places.

High Court of Australia *Parliament House*

looking across the

In the preparation of this book I gathered a wealth of material (sadly not all of which could be used) and express my gratitude to all those who assisted with its acquisition. I would like particularly to thank the Canberra Historical Society; the Embassies of Austria, United States of America, Belgium, Brazil, Republic of Chile, Denmark, Arab Republic of Egypt, Finland, Greece, Hungarian People's Republic, Indonesia, Israel, Islamic Republic of Iran, Japan, Lao People's Democratic Republic, Lebanon, Socialist People's Libyan Arab Jamahiriya, United Mexican States, Royal Netherlands, Pakistan, Philippines, Peru, Polish People's Republic, Portugal, South Africa, Spain, Turkey, Republic of Venezuela, Socialist Federal Republic of Yugoslavia; the High Commissions of Britain, Canada, Republic of Cyprus, Fiji, Ghana, Malaysia, New Zealand, and Singapore.

Many of the recipes in this book were generously contributed by Canberra residents. The source of these recipes is acknowledged in the index, where the name of the contributor follows the recipe which he or she provided. Thanks are due to Virginia Moore, Dot McMahon, Jeanette Clarke, Helen Tanner, Jane Southwell, Pat Baxter, Cynthia Gullick, Vyner Law, Pat Guest, Lady Mary Scholtens, Maureen Woods, Mim Hunt, Carol-Anne Macaulay, Nelly Haycock, Mary Cousins, George Warwick-Smith, Pat

Treasury Building   National Library.
Burley-Griffin, towards the Brindabellas.

Reithmuller, Jann Vaughan, Heather Lloyd, Eleanor Stirling, Kerry Webb, Colleen Hackett, Peter Hackett, Karin Russell, Shirly Lutze, Margot Anthony, Martha Wiederman, Harry Markaulli, Kevin Wilson, John Moore, Carole Castle, Bob Sykes, Anne Robson, Anne Loveridge, Shirley Larson, Pat Heffernan, Shirley Meldrum, Eunice Alexander, Doug McKay, Margaret Morrison, C.C. Halton, Margaret Swain, Norma Sivertsen, Gwen Moseley, Ellen Gustavsen, Jim Scully, Wilma McKeown, Dr Gwyn Howells, Mary Stannard, Dawn Scutts, Sue Baxter, Dorothy Lyons, W.B. Pritchett, Anne McKernan, Helen Alwyn, June Slocum, Ingrid Murphy, Laurie Daniels, Noeline Garty, Esdene Richter, Mary Dodds, Margaret Dalton, Vee Longworth, June Barbour, Denise Markaulli, Edna Boling, M.A. Besley, Jean Frost, Jean Townsend, Sir Richard Kingsland, L. Savage, Viv Ashcroft, Tamie Fraser, Peter Lawler, Sir Geoffrey Yeend, Gloria Steward, Bev Curlewis, Ron Driver, Rona Quinn, Joyce Bulgagier, Linda Kellam, Jan Bowling, Shirley Larson, Dorothy Powell, Meg Morrow, Colleen Brazil.

I would also like to thank the restaurants that contributed recipes to the book: Bacchus Tavern, the Lobby Restaurant, the Carousel, E. J.s, Black Mountain Tower Restaurant, the Village Chef, Zanna's, Nobb's. Special thanks to journalists Alan Fitzgerald, Rowena Stretton and Max Harris.

Bell Tower, Puntroon

* O·L·D T·I·M·E·R·S *

Here is a selection of recipes — sometimes written 'receipts' — from days gone by. All were contributed by Canberra residents whose ancestors settled the area.

This section, then, is dedicated to those whose families struggled for survival in what was in the early twentieth century merely a tiny isolated inland settlement.

SODA BREAD

Mix together in a bowl:
6 cups plain flour
1 teaspoon bicarbonate of soda
1 teaspoon salt
Make a well in the centre and add *1 cup sour milk (or fresh milk or buttermilk)* to make a thick dough. (If fresh milk is used, *1 teaspoon cream of tartar* should be added to flour mixture.)
Dough mixture should be slack but not wet. Add a little more milk if too stiff.
Put on lightly floured board and flatten with floured hands into a circle about 3.5 cm (1½ inches) thick
Cut across dough (making a cross) and bake in moderate to hot oven (190°–200°C) for about 40 minutes.
When baked, wrap in clean tea towel to cool.

BLUNDELL'S FARMHOUSE

This attractive stone and slab cottage stands on the banks of Lake Burley Griffin — once the site of extensive farmland — and serves as a reminder of Canberra's pastoral beginning. Its surroundings have changed dramatically and to understand its original background one must visualise the Molonglo River, fringed with willows, meandering along a course down the centre of the river flats — now the depths of Lake Burley Griffin.

The cottage was built in 1858 by Robert Campbell for one of his employees, William Ginn, who, with his family, arrived in Sydney from Hertfordshire late in 1857. Under the tenancy, William Ginn was allowed to farm an area of 20 hectares attached to the house.

Three children were born at the cottage before the Ginns moved in the late 1860s to their own selection a few kilometres away. That area is now known as Ginn's Gap.

William (1821–1904) and his wife Mary (1824–1917) are buried in St John the Baptist churchyard nearby, and descendants of the family still live in the Canberra district.

The second occupants of the farmhouse were George and Flora Blundell, who lived there for more than fifty years. George was Robert Campbell's bullock driver. Nine children were born there, and so were some grandchildren. Admittedly the house was twice extended! Descendants of the family still live in the district.

There was a short tenancy by Mr and Mrs Walton, followed by Henry and Alice Oldfield in 1932. After the death of her husband in 1942, Mrs Oldfield continued to live in the cottage until her death in 1958.

In 1964 Blundell's Farmhouse was handed over to the Canberra and District Historical Society. The cottage has been preserved and restored and contains six small rooms. In keeping with the cottage's historical atmosphere there are no electricity, water or sewerage services. The old-fashioned flowers in the garden also reflect the cottage's past.

Blundell's Farmhouse is open for inspection daily.

Blundell's Farmhouse.

AUSTRALIA CAKE

This was on a page torn from the *Australian Women's Weekly* dated 27 March 1937.

6 oz butter,
6 oz sugar
3 eggs
6 tablespoons milk
12 oz self-raising flour
vanilla
cochineal
raspberry jam

Cream butter and sugar, add beaten eggs, then milk and essence, lastly sifted flour. Put half into well-greased 7-inch square cake tin. Spread with jam. Colour remainder pink, and spread over jam. Bake in a moderate oven about 60 minutes. Turn out carefully. Ice if liked when cold.

Helen Tanner's grandfather, William Jardine, came to Australia from Scotland in 1841. He found his way to the Monaro from Sydney in 1846 and became one of the district's best known pioneers.

William Jardine started a flour mill at Jindabyne in partnership with Stewart Ryrie jnr — the motive power being the waters of the Snowy River — and worked this for a number of years.

In 1852 he married Scots-born Cathrane Cochrane. They had five children.

Over the years William Jardine acquired several holdings and particularly devoted himself to the improvement of Curry Flat, transforming it into a holding favourable to sheep breeding and wool growing. Curry Flat is still in the Jardine family.

APPLE CHUTNEY

From a handwritten recipe book compiled by Cathrane Cochrane.

10 large cooking apples
5 onions (sliced)
3 cups stoned raisins
2 lb dark sugar
1½ bottles vinegar
1 tablespoon mustard
1 tablespoon black pepper
1 tablespoon salt
1 tablespoon cayenne pepper

Mix all together and boil well. Bottle and make airtight.

Buggy lamp.

'A lady's taste and nicety are very perceptible at the breakfast table. She should never allow a soiled tablecloth to appear on it. The linen should be fresh and snowy white, the silver brightly cleaned, the tea, coffee, or cocoa nicely made, and, if possible, fresh flowers and fruit should adorn the table. A nicely laid, pretty, appetising breakfast is a good promoter of good temper and harmony through the ensuing day.'

The Ladies' Treasury, 1868

Rosevale, a farmhouse just off the Barton Highway and only about five kilometres from the Civic Centre, is alive with history. Bought from the Malone family by newlyweds John and Jane Southwell in 1917, it had five rooms and was made of pesi (mostly mud and roughage), a cheap building material.

John and Jane had three children, two boys and a girl, and stayed at the farm until 1976. Jane recalls that it was 1946 before electricity came through the area and they were carting water until then.

In the early 1920s Rosevale property was also the site of the Ainslie Cricket Club. Close by the farmhouse was a huge box tree which provided shelter for the cricketers and their gear, which they transported to the site in large boxes.

Perhaps more importantly, the box tree provided shade for the enjoyment of the customary afternoon tea — a greatly enjoyed break in the afternoon. All the womenfolk brought food and swapped recipes and the tree became affectionately known as 'The Cricket Box Tree'.

One of the best remembered afternoon tea donations was brought along by a Mrs Stone whose husband and brothers were all keen cricketers. The cake was much enjoyed by everybody and the recipe was quickly exchanged. It is still very popular in the area.

AUNT NELLY'S SAGO PLUM PUDDING

A very old recipe

1 cup sago soaked in *milk* overnight. (Cover sago well with milk — better soaked about lunchtime).

Mix in:

1 cup breadcrumbs
¾ cup raisins and currants
1 tablespoon golden syrup or treacle
1 tablespoon butter
1 teaspoon bicarbonate of soda

Steam 2½ to 3 hours.

(Just mix the butter through — don't cream.)

MRS STONE'S SPICED APPLE CAKE

Always use a breakfast cup for measurements — not a small teacup.

Cream:

90 g (3 oz) butter
½ breakfast cup sugar

Add:

1 egg, and beat well

Mix in these dry ingredients sifted twice:

1 breakfast cup plain flour
1 teaspoon baking powder
2 teaspoons cinnamon
2 teaspoons allspice
2 teaspoons ginger

Turn out onto a lightly floured board and knead into a nice smooth ball.

Divide the mixture into two, pressing half into a 20 cm (8 inch) sandwich tin, greased and lined with greaseproof paper. Cover this with a layer of cold stewed apple.

Roll out the second layer and cover the apple. (Don't worry if it falls about and breaks up, just get it on the best way you can and it'll all join up in the cooking process. It's easier to do this in the cold weather.)

Bake in a fairly hot oven (200°C) for 35–40 minutes.

When cool, ice with lemon icing and when cold cut into bars.

A Fireless Cooker

'1 butter box, sufficient floral cretonne to make 2 pillows to fit in box nicely, fill pillows with chaff. Paint butter box to match your kitchen, stand on four legs, now put a pillow of chaff in box. Bring to the boil anything such as stews, currys, etc. or anything that needs cooking for hours. Put in box, making a hole in pillow with saucepan. Put the other pillow on top, making the box full in all. Put on the lid and it will remain at boiling point for hours and hours. Excellent for preparing baby's food, and very handy if going out for the afternoon and putting on a hot tea.'

CWA Coronation Cookery Book, 1937

DUNTROON HOUSE

This gracious old homestead — today the officers' mess of Australia's Royal Military College, Duntroon — was built by Sydney merchant, Robert Campbell.

The original house was the single-storeyed south wing of the present building, built in 1833. It was a square cottage surrounded by a verandah and it may have had a detached kitchen and servants' quarters behind.

Campbell himself didn't live there, though he visited occasionally and died there in 1840. On Campbell's death the property which, until then, was run by his overseer, James Ainslie, passed to his fourth son, George. It was actually managed by the third son, Charles, until George married in 1854 and took up residence.

In 1862, extensions to the homestead commenced, and the two-storeyed wing and servants' quarters were built. New stables, lodges and other buildings followed. The beautiful gardens, too, were established during this time. Rumour has it that George Campbell planted a tree from every country he visited. Duntroon House was the centre of life for the family and for the many station employees.

While the Campbells ruled in the strict Victorian manner they were noted for their generosity and for their attention to the welfare of their employees.

George Campbell died in 1881 and his widow remained at Duntroon until her death in 1903.

In 1910, Colonel Bridges selected Duntroon as the site for the military college. The house and 150 hectares of land were leased and later purchased from George Campbell's heir. In recent years there have been some alterations internally but the original woodwork — mostly cedar — remains intact.

The charter of the Royal Military College requires it to train cadets 'in the service of the crown' as officers in the Australian Army. It demands that the course of instruction should 'promote a sense of honour and loyalty, duty and responsibility; inculcate habits of discipline and soldierly conduct; and give a correct understanding of the place of the Armed Services in the Australian nation'.

As a former Commandant said: 'Our job is to produce good soldiers who are also well-educated men.'

Runtroon House.

LEMON SYRUP

A very old recipe — easy, quick, economical and thirst quenching
Dissolve *2 cups sugar* in *2 cups boiling water*.
Add *1½ teaspoons tartaric acid* and *1 teaspoon lemon essence*.

Jeannette Clarke's family lives at Emu Flat in Braidwood, 40 kilometres south of the Shoalhaven River. Jeannette's father, James Dempsey, was born there, the property having been a government grant to an ancestor, Cornelius Dempsey, in 1838.

Cornelius' father, James Dempsey, a stonemason, began life in the colony of New South Wales as a convict, arriving in Sydney on the second voyage of the ship *Atlas* with over 100 other Irish deportees. The year was 1802. James Dempsey was given a free pardon in 1811 and later purchased land in Sydney's Rocks area.

Jeannette Clarke's paternal grandmother was a Hindmarsh, whose family migrated from England to the Braidwood area. She had the reputation of being an outstanding cook. This is one of her recipes.

CURRANT BISCUITS

4 cups flour
1 cup butter
1 cup sugar
2 teaspoons baking powder
currants, dates or sultanas
Rub butter into flour, add other ingredients, mix with *milk* into stiff dough. Bake in a moderate oven.

flat iron.

MRS GREY'S MINT CHUTNEY

Pound together:
2 *tablespoons chopped mint*
2 *tablespoons seeded raisins*
Add:
salt to taste and a *pinch of cayenne*
Put in a saucepan:
1 *tablespoon vinegar*
1 *tablespoon sugar*
Boil a few minutes then pour over the mint mixture.
Bottle when cold and use instead of mint sauce.

When the Southern Tablelands explorer Charles Throsby heard about the existence of Lake George he sent his overseer to find it. That man was Joseph Wild, already over sixty and an excellent bushman.

His story is a fascinating one, as related by his great-great-granddaughter, Mrs Linda Kellam, who lives in Spence, ACT.

Joseph Wild was a Londoner who came to Australia as a convict in the early 1800s. When Throsby 'found' him, he was in charge of a road gang making a track through to Goulburn from Sydney. He was given special leave to assist Throsby on his expedition and proved to be the mainstay on many future expeditions.

Wild was later given a grant of land near Appin where he lived with his family until his death at the age of eighty-eight — resulting from a confrontation with a wild bull!

Wilde's Meadow, although spelt differently, is named after him, and there are unconfirmed reports that he was the first police constable in the district.

Joseph Wild had a fixation about King George, after whom he named both the lake and his eldest son.

While it is acknowledged that Wild's education was minimal, he was apparently a most intelligent man who assisted Throsby in dictating reports which were sent to London. All his letters were published by the London *Times*.

Mrs Linda Kellam, great-great-granddaughter of the Southern Tablelands pioneer, Joseph Wild, was born in 1905 at Lockhart in New South Wales. When she was twelve her mother died and Linda and her four siblings went to live with her grandparents on a wheat farm at Lake Albert. She affectionately and appreciatively recalls her grandmother, Eliza Jane, rearing these children in addition to twelve of her own!

During the big drought of 1905, Grandma Wild is credited with having invented a recipe for a cake/biscuit called 'Hard Times'. They were thicker and bigger than biscuits, and consisted of dripping, sugar, eggs, flour, milk, bicarbonate of soda and cream of tartar. (They couldn't afford baking powder!)

Sometimes 'Hard Times' had currants in them, sometimes lemon peel. Grandma Wild mixed the ingredients to a dough, then spread it onto a large floured board with her hands and cut it into rounds.

This is another family recipe.

FAMILY FAVOURITE SPONGE CAKE

Beat *4 eggs* until frothy, then add, gradually, *1 cup sugar*, taking 15 minutes to beat it all in.

Next, fold in *1 cup self-raising flour*, using a wooden spoon.

Finally, stir in *1 dessertspoon butter*, melted and mixed with *4 tablespoons boiling water*.

Pour the mixture into 2 × 20 cm (8 inch) greased and floured sandwich tins and bake in a hot oven (220°C) for 15 minutes. Cool on a rack.

Try a raspberry jam and cream filling and top with passionfruit icing.

'O Woman, woman! Take my advice and learn to cook. Then shall your gentle ministration be as sweet savour in the nostrils of your husband, and your labour be acceptable unto him even when you have had fourteen children. Teach all your girls to cook, and you shall be blessed even by the generation that comes after you.'

Chambers Journal, 1868

TOMATO SAUCE

Boil together for 4 hours:
6 kg (12 lb) tomatoes, chopped
125 g (4 oz) salt
750 g (1½ lb) sugar
500 g (1 lb) apples, washed and chopped (use peel and core too)
3 large onions, chopped
1 teaspoon cayenne pepper
600 ml (1 pint) vinegar
1 dessertspoon white pepper ⎱
1 tablespoon allspice   tied in a
30 g (1 oz) whole cloves ⎰ muslin bag

Strain through a sieve, and cork when cold.

Note: In the old days, spices were available whole and the original recipe called for whole allspice and whole cloves. While the latter are still readily available, you can use the ground variety if you wish.

TOMATO AND PINEAPPLE JAM

This recipe was found in the back of an old recipe book. This is exactly as it was written.

6 lb tomatoes
1 pineapple
4½ lb sugar
1 small teaspoon tartaric acid

Plunge the tomatoes into boiling water a few minutes and the skins will easily peel off. Cut a good sized pineapple into small dice, boil together with 1 lb of sugar for about 20 minutes.

While it is boiling heat the rest of the sugar in the oven for a little and when hot, add to the boiling jam.

Boil all quickly ¾ of an hour or longer. A few minutes before taking off, add the tartaric acid.

I never go exactly by the time, but just boil till a little put on a saucer to cool begins to wrinkle.

I got some good big tomatoes for 4 pence a pound last week — a pineapple for 6 pence. As the sugar is only 10 pence — it is quite an economical jam — as it made about 10 shillings worth.

heanyou Homestead
from main access road.
Resumed by the
federal Government
in 1971
Open to the public
since 1975.

LANYON

Lanyon property, near Tharwa, was named after John Lanyon who, with James Wright, settled in the area in the early 1830s. They were free settlers from Derby in England, and when James's brother William joined them they held an area of 1932 hectacres adjoining the Murrumbidgee River. The area was then known as Jegalite.

In 1837 William accidentally shot himself and was buried in the Lanyon cemetery. John Lanyon returned to England, leaving James Wright to run the property.

Convicts who were assigned to James built many of the outbuildings still standing today.

Before James married in 1838 he built a permanent homestead in the same style as the old kitchen block. This homestead occupied the site of the present guest wing and was demolished in the 1880s. Wright was forced to sell Lanyon in 1847 and moved to Cuppacumbalong.

Andrew and Jane Cunningham came to Australia with their three children in 1845, and moved to Lanyon in 1847. Cunningham leased the property after Wright's foreclosure and

gradually acquired blocks until, in 1859, he built a new homestead.

Andrew Cunningham quickly became one of the district's most influential people. He and his wife had four sons and four daughters. Two sons, Andrew Jackson and James, inherited Lanyon and James and his wife took up residence there. When the partnership dissolved about 1908, Andrew Jackson took up Lanyon and James kept all the remaining local properties.

Andrew died in 1913 and in 1915 James and his family returned to Lanyon. The Osborne family bought it in 1926 and by 1930 it had passed to the pastoralist Thomas Field. The Fields recognised Lanyon's historical value.

Lanyon was one of the ACT's larger freehold properties when it was resumed by the government in 1971. The homestead was opened to the public as a gallery from 1975 to 1979 and a collection of Sidney Nolan's paintings, which had been given to the people of Australia, was established there. In 1980 the Nolan Gallery was set up in a timber building nearby.

Lanyon homestead has been furnished with items borrowed from the National Trust of Australia (ACT).

NANA MUN'S GREEN TOMATO PICKLES

Wash, trim and dice *2 kg (4 lb) green tomatoes* and peel and dice *6 large onions.*

Put in a heavy saucepan or boiler, sprinkle over *½ cup cooking salt* and leave overnight.

In the morning drain off liquid.

Add:

1 tablespoon whole black peppercorns ⎱ tied in a
1 tablespoon cloves ⎰ muslin bag

Cover the mixture with *brown vinegar* and boil gently until tender.

Then stir in *1 kg (2 lb) sugar.*

In a small bowl mix:

2 tablespoons cornflour
2 tablespoons mustard
2 tablespoons curry powder
½ teaspoon cayenne pepper

Add enough water to mix to a thin paste and stir into the tomato mixture.

Cook 15 minutes to thicken.

Before bottling (hot) remove the muslin bag.

* D·I·P·L·O·M·A·T·S' D·I·S·H·E·S *

How fortunate we are to have so many countries represented in our national capital. Canberra is of course the centre for diplomatic missions and this section is devoted to their generous contributions.

HIGH COMMISSION OF CANADA

PRESSED HAM

You'll need *a large shoulder of pork*, put in a boiler with:
2 cups of beer
2 bayleaves
1 tablespoon dry mustard
4 tablespoons molasses
Simmer until very well cooked and let cool in the juice.
Then pour off the juice, take the bone out and press the meat in a mould.

BRITISH HIGH COMMISSION

TREACLE TART

You'll need *250 g (8 oz) sweet or rich shortcrust pastry*
Use ⅔ of the pastry to line a 20 cm (8 inch) pie plate. Spread over it *250 g (8 oz) golden syrup* and on top of that *1 cup white breadcrumbs* mixed with the grated rind and juice of *1 lemon*, plus *a pinch of ginger* and *cinnamon*.

EMBASSY OF PAKISTAN

SOME INTERESTING ASPECTS OF PAKISTANI CUISINE:

• It is considered improper to make anything too hotly flavoured; rather, cooks rely on subtleties of flavour.

• Coconut is never used.

• Silver foil, exceptionally fine, is used as a decoration for both sweet and savoury dishes instead of nuts, chocolate shavings, etc. According to local lore it is very good for the heart.

• Curries are never served with accompaniments such as coconut, sultanas or nuts — they ruin a good curry!

PASANDA CURRY

In a pan or cast-iron casserole with *125 g (4 oz) heated cooking fat (or butter)* brown *2 medium onions*, sliced.
Add:
1 kg (2 lb) undercut of beef or veal, cut into 2 cm (¾ inch) thick slices
125 g (4 oz) plain yoghurt
4 dried red chillies (or 2 teaspoons powder)
8 cloves garlic, finely sliced
2 pieces fresh ginger, finely sliced (*or ½ teaspoon powder*)
salt to taste
Cook on slow heat until tender and most of the liquid has been reduced.
Serve with vegetable rice.
Serves 6.

'A cook should never be retained who is not fond of her occupation: for unless she takes pleasure in her art, she cannot be depended upon for accuracy in the preparation of dishes with which she is well acquainted, and, moreover, will not easily be induced to learn anything new.'

Tasmanian Home Cookery, 1850

'If orders be given early in the morning; there will be more time to execute them; and servants by doing their work without hurry and bustle, will be more likely to do it well, and fewer will be necessary.'

Tasmanian Home Cookery, 1850

EMBASSY OF BRAZIL

FEIJAO BRANCO ASSADO
(Brazilian Baked Beans)

Soak *500 g (1 lb) dry white beans* overnight. Drain, add water to cover and cook with:

500 g (1 lb) breast of lamb, cubed with as much fat cut away as possible
500 g (1 lb) smoked ham or tongue
1 bayleaf

Simmer until meats are tender and beans are cooked.

In a pan fry *250 g (8 oz) bacon*, cubed, then drain off most of the fat.

Put in *½ cup chopped onions* and saute them. Then add:

1 cup peeled, chopped fresh tomatoes
(or *1 cup tomato sauce*)
1 garlic clove, crushed
salt and *pepper* to taste

Simmer for 10 minutes then add to the bean mixture.

Continue to simmer the lot for another 40 to 50 minutes, taste and correct the seasoning.

Now, pour a third of the beans into a buttered casserole and place the pieces of meat on top, then add the rest of the beans.

Sprinkle *breadcrumbs* on top, dot with *butter* and bake in a moderate oven (190°C) for 10 minutes.

Serves 6–8.

EMBASSY OF THE UNITED STATES OF AMERICA

SPICED PICKLED SHRIMP

This hors d'oeuvre comes from South Georgia. It's very easy and very good.

You'll need:

1 kg (2 lb) prawns
6 small white onions

In a crockpot put a layer of prawns, a layer of *bayleaves*, then a layer of onions.

Alternate until all the prawns are used.

Mix all these ingredients in a pan:

4 tablespoons olive oil
2 tablespoons tarragon vinegar
½ teaspoon salt
½ teaspoon dry mustard
cayenne pepper
½ teaspoon powdered sugar
handful of pickling spices

Pour over the prawns and leave in the fridge for at least 24 hours.

Stir occasionally and add lemon juice and salt if needed.

Serve with toothpicks in a bowl over ice on a bed of lettuce.

ROYAL BELGIAN EMBASSY

CHICKEN WATERZOIE

This is a speciality from the region of Ghent.
Use a *boiling fowl*, and rub it over with *one lemon*.
Put in a pot with:
2 *onions, stuck with a few cloves*
3 *sticks celery*, chopped
3 *leeks*, sliced
1 *medium carrot*, sliced
just enough *water* to cover
Bring to the boil and add:
a *bouquet garni* (a mixture of herbs tied securely in a piece of material)
½ *bottle white wine*
salt and *pepper*
Simmer for 1½ hours.
To serve, cut the chicken into pieces, remove the bouquet garni, and serve the chicken in the stock with the vegetables, garnished with chopped parsley.
Serves 4–6.

EMBASSY OF THE REPUBLIC OF CHILE

CREME DE ABACATE
(Avocado Cream)

Put in an electric blender or food processor (in 2 or 3 lots):
the flesh of 2 *large ripe avocados*
3 *tablespoons lime juice (or 2 teaspoons lemon juice)*
4 *tablespoons icing sugar*
When smooth, put small portions in individual glass serving dishes, or glasses, and top each dish with a thin slice of *lemon* or *lime*.
Serves 4.

THE AUSTRALIAN WAR MEMORIAL

Opened in 1941 during World War II, this cream sandstone structure stands as a memorial to Australians who served in times of war. It is the nation's memorial to their sacrifices and achievements.

The War Memorial owes its origin to an idea put forward by Dr C. E. W. Bean, official war historian with the Australians in World War I. In 1917 he persuaded Sir William Birdwood, GOC of the AIF, to establish a War Records Section, and it was not long before it was working in every area where Australians were engaged. Troops — including among them some of Australia's best known artists — responded willingly to requests to participate. Many more artists and photographers were recruited.

When in 1925 an Act of Parliament was passed to establish the Australian War Memorial, a vast collection had been acquired. By the time the building opened in 1941 it was clear that extensions would be necessary. Two wings were added between 1968 and 1971.

The Memorial stands in a large area of terraced lawns on the lower southern slopes of Mt Ainslie. From the front entrance there is a magnificent view looking down Anzac Parade across Lake Burley Griffin to Parliament House and the Brindabella Range beyond. The building is cruciform in shape and is topped by a huge copper dome under which is situated the famous central shrine, the Hall of Memory.

A brief visit to the Memorial is impossible: there is too much to see. Visitors spend hours in what is recognised as a shrine, a museum, an art gallery and a repository of priceless records.

Unique among the world's great national monuments, the Australian War Memorial attracts more visitors — over half a million a year — than any other attraction in Canberra.

The Australian War
Memorial

EMBASSY OF INDONESIA

GADO GADO
(Cooked Salad)

In boiling salted water cook:
1–2 *carrots*
2–3 *medium potatoes*
Drain and set aside to cool.

Cook *250 g (8 oz) beans*, chopped, and *¼ medium cabbage*, shredded, either by boiling in salted water for a short while or by frying gently in a little butter with a shaking of salt.

Now, line a serving dish with *lettuce leaves*. Arrange layers of cabbage, potato (sliced), carrot rings, beans and *250 g (8 oz) bean shoots* and garnish with:
2 medium tomatoes, cut into chunks
1 medium cucumber, sliced
2 hard-boiled eggs, sliced or quartered
½ cup crisp fried onion flakes
Serve with Peanut Sauce.
Serves 4.

PEANUT SAUCE

In a pan saute:
½ teaspoon chopped garlic (or ¼ teaspoon garlic powder)
4 tablespoons peanut butter
1 teaspoon chilli powder
1 bayleaf
1 thin slice lemon
After a few minutes add gradually *1 cup water* mixed with *½ cup milk*, or *coconut milk*, or *2 tablespoons fine desiccated coconut*.

Add *salt* to taste and cook on low heat, stirring continuously until the mixture thickens.

EMBASSY OF JAPAN

CHAWAN-MUSHI
(Steamed Egg Custard)

Lightly beat *4 eggs* (don't over-beat so as to make bubbles in the mixture).

Fold through:

400 ml (⅔ pt) fish stock
1½ teaspoons soy sauce
1 teaspoon salt
1 teaspoon sweet sake (mirin)
¼ teaspoon monosodium glutamate

Shell *6 prawns*, chop *2 large mushrooms* (if using dried Japanese mushrooms they should be soaked in lukewarm water until they become soft) and remove the stems.

Chop or shred *50 g (nearly 2 oz) chicken* (make sure the mushroom pieces and chicken pieces are the same size).

Put a *large spinach leaf* (or 2 smaller ones, or enough to tear into 6 pieces to fit in each bowl) into *boiling water* for several seconds, then soak in *cold water* and squeeze out excess water from the leaf.

Now, place the prawns, some chicken, mushrooms, spinach and *ginko nuts** (2 in each bowl) into 6 individual ovenproof serving bowls, and add to them equal quantities of the egg mixture.

Place the bowls in a hot steamer. Before steaming, place greaseproof paper under the lid of the steamer to prevent moisture dripping into the cups.

Steam for approximately 15 minutes at a constant low heat (if it's too hot the custard will curdle).

To test that the custard is set, dip a thin skewer into the mixture. If a clear liquid runs out, the custard is cooked and should be served while hot.

Serves 6

**Note: Ginko nuts are available in tins in many Asian food stores.*

JAPANESE EMBASSY

Although not representative of any specific style or phase in Japanese history and not modelled on any outstanding ancient structure, the Japanese Embassy includes many types of traditional architecture and contains features and materials found in traditional Japanese buildings.

The building was designed by the Architecture and Engineering Division of the Japanese Foreign Ministry in collaboration with the Australian architects, Grounds, Romberg & Boyd. It was constructed by A. V. Jennings Construction Co. Pty Ltd in 1961.

Japanese buildings were traditionally made of wood, a material which placed limits on their style and shape and, particularly, on their height. The Embassy is made of reinforced concrete but has exposed beams, pillars and handrails along the verandahs that give the effect and atmosphere of a traditional wooden residence.

It also features wide windows, another characteristic of traditional Japanese buildings. Their inclusion in modern buildings has been made possible by the use of reinforced concrete. The original purpose was to blend interior space with the exterior. To increase this effect, the eaves were extended and the floor so arranged that the external garden was brought in under the eaves.

The Embassy gardens comprise two styles that are typical of traditional Japanese gardens. First, while not representative of any particular historic garden, they contain features to be found in a traditional tea garden. The Japanese tea garden, introduced about 400 years ago, usually included a tea house set close to a pond. It was reached by one or more footpaths designed for strolling through the garden. This type of garden has a dual purpose: to satisfy aesthetically and to provide repose.

Second, the gardens owe their style to Zen Buddhism and to the art of Sumie or Indian ink painting, both of which were imported from China.

The Embassy gardens were planned by the Ixda Zoen Jimusho, Tokyo.

Embassy of Japan.

HIGH COMMISSION OF MALAYSIA

BEEF RENDANG

In a casserole over low heat, heat *4 tablespoons cooking oil* until slightly smoking.

Put in these blended ingredients and fry until fragrant:
10 dried chillies
10 black peppercorns
2.5 cm (1 inch) ginger
5 cloves garlic
5 onions
4 tablespoons dried lemon grass (or 2 teaspoons powdered lemon grass)
1 candlenut (or Brazil nut or macadamia nut)

Next, add:
1 kg (2 lb) beef, cut into medium-sized pieces
salt to taste

Fry another 2 to 3 minutes.

Add:
250 g (8 oz) creamed coconut
4 cups water

Simmer over very low heat until the curry is quite dry. Stir constantly and don't let the curry boil!

Add:
juice of *1 lime* and
1 pinch turmeric
and cook another 1 or 2 minutes.

Serve very hot.

Serves 4–6.

'The careful direction of her table is no small part of a lady's duties; it involves judgement in expenditure, a thorough knowledge of cooking and regard for appearance; the comfort of her husband as well as those who partake of her hospitality depends on it.'

Tasmanian Home Cookery, 1850

EMBASSY OF THE UNITED MEXICAN STATES

GUACAMOLE

Guacamole is almost a must in a Mexican meal. It is used as a complement for hot tortillas, rice and meat.

Mash the flesh of 3 *avocados* with a wooden spoon.

Roast, skin and grind (a blender will do the job well) 2 *tomatoes* with 1 *onion*, chopped, and 1 *chilli*, chopped finely.

Add this mixture to the mashed avocados.

Mix in:

1 tablespoon *chopped coriander* (if fresh is unavailable use dried coriander)

2 tablespoons *olive oil*

salt and *pepper*

Put the avocado pits in the sauce until serving time.

This may be served as a dip.

HIGH COMMISSION OF NEW ZEALAND

CHILLED TOHEROA AND ZUCCHINI SOUP

Because toheroas (small molluscs) are found only on certain protected beaches in New Zealand and can be dug by hand for a very short season each year, they are a greatly prized delicacy. Fortunately, they are exported in soup form, though in limited quantities.

Cook 1 *large onion*, sliced, in 1 *tablespoon butter* for 5 minutes. Add 9 *trimmed and sliced zucchinis* and 1 *level teaspoon salt* and cook for a few minutes longer before adding 1 *cup water*.

Simmer for about 10 minutes, cool slightly then put in a blender until the mixture is smooth.

Stir in 1 *tin toheroa soup*, bring to the boil, then remove from the heat and add 1 *tin evaporated milk* and ½ *cup fresh cream*.

Serve chilled, with a dob of *sour cream* on top.

Serves 8.

GOVERNMENT HOUSE, YARRALUMLA

This building was originally Yarralumla Homestead and stood on a property owned by Terence Aubrey Murray, who lived in the house from 1837 until 1858. In that year his wife died and as the property was in her name, she willed it to her father and brother. The latter, Augustus Gibbs, took over Yarralumla the same year.

Murray's life was much altered by these events. He took his children and moved to his Windareen estate. In 1860 he married Agnes, his children's governess. The following year Agnes gave birth to a son, John Hubert Plunkett Murray, who was later to become famous as Sir Hubert Murray, Administrator of Papua New Guinea. A second son, George Gilbert Murray, became an eminent Oxford classicist.

Terence Murray received a knighthood in 1869 but, because of his inability to pay his creditors, he had lost Windareen. With the loss of both his pastoral properties and his reduced financial circumstances his health deteriorated, and he died in 1873 at the age of sixty-three.

In 1881 Murray's brother-in-law, Augustus Gibbs, sold the Yarralumla property to Frederick Campbell, who extended the homestead in 1891. In 1911, when the Federal Capital Territory came into existence, the Australian Government acquired the property. The homestead was renovated and in 1927 it began to be used as a vice-regal residence.

Twenty-eight Governors-General or Administrators have been in residence in the years since then. Of the thirteen Governors-General seven — including the present incumbent, Sir Ninian Stephen — have been Australian-born.

EMBASSY OF THE PHILIPPINES

CHICKEN AND PORK ADOBO

Adobo is the national dish of the Philippines.

In a saucepan combine:

½ *cup vinegar*

2 *cloves garlic*, crushed or finely chopped

1 *bayleaf*

¼ *teaspoon black pepper*

1–4 *teaspoons soy sauce*

500 *g (1 lb) pork fillet*, cut into equal-sized pieces

Let it all boil until the pork is half cooked, then add *one large chicken* cut into equal-sized pieces.

Let it boil again until the pork and chicken are quite tender.

Strain the sauce and set it aside.

Now, fry the chicken and pork in very hot *cooking oil*, until brownish in colour. Return the meat to the saucepan, pour the sauce over, then cover and simmer until the sauce thickens.

Serve hot.

Serves 6.

EMBASSY OF LEBANON

EGGPLANT IN OIL

Peel 2 *kg (4 lb) eggplants* and cut them into large pieces. Fry lightly in 200 *g (6½ oz) heated oil* in a pan, and then remove them from the pan.

In the same oil fry 400 *g (13 oz) small whole onions*.

Into a heavy-based saucepan or cast-iron casserole, put the onions, together with 600 *g (1¼ lb) ripe tomatoes*, peeled, seeded and chopped. Arrange the eggplant pieces on top, sprinkle with *salt* and *pepper* and top with another 600 *g (1¼ lb) tomatoes* prepared as before.

Simmer gently, covered, until cooked. Transfer to a serving dish and refrigerate when cooled. Serve cold.

Serves 6.

'One of the most important acquisitions in the routine of daily life is the ability to carve, not only well, but elegantly. It is true that the present fashion of Russian dinners is fast banishing the necessity for promiscuous carving from the richly served boards of the wealthy; but in the circles of middle life, where it is not adopted, the necessity of skill in the use of a carving knife is sufficiently obvious.

'The dish upon which the article to be carved is placed should be conveniently near to the carver so that he may have full control over it; for if it is placed too far off, nothing can prevent an ungracefulness of appearance, and a difficulty in performing that which if it were in its proper place could be achieved with ease.'

Mary Jewry, *Model Cookery and Housekeeping Book.*

EMBASSY OF THE POLISH PEOPLE'S REPUBLIC

RICE, MUSHROOMS AND MEAT AU GRATIN

Grease a heavy saucepan or cast-iron casserole with *1 tablespoon butter* and sprinkle the base with *a tablespoon of breadcrumbs.*

In a pan melt *1½ tablespoons butter* and in it cook *200 g (6 oz) onions*, chopped finely. When soft add:

500 g (1 lb) mushrooms, peeled and finely sliced

Stir occasionally and when soft add:

250 g (8 oz) roast beef (cooked rare), cut into small strips

Cook separately *250 g (8 oz) rice* in boiling, salted water until tender (about 20 minutes). Drain and rinse in cold water.

Now, mix the boiled rice with the mushroom/onion/meat mixture.

Season to taste with *salt* and *pepper.*

Mix in *2 eggs* and transfer the lot to the buttered casserole dish. Smooth the top and bake in a moderate oven until very hot — 20 to 30 minutes.

Serve with a hot sauce and green salad.

Serves 6.

SOUTH AFRICAN EMBASSY

BOBOTIE

Soak *1 slice crustless bread* in *300 ml (½ pint) milk*.

Mince or chop finely *500 g (1 lb) mutton or beef* and put it in a heavy casserole dish. Add *¾ cup water* and simmer gently on the stove for 15 minutes.

In another pan melt *½ tablespoon butter* and when sizzling add *1 medium onion*, chopped, and cook until it browns.

Now, add to the meat:
the fried onion
1 tablespoon raisins
1 tablespoon curry powder
the bread (just the bread, keep any remaining milk for the custard)
1 teaspoon mango chutney
4–8 almonds, chopped
¾ cup beef stock (can be made with a cube)
1 dessertspoon lemon juice
Season carefully with *salt*.

For the custard, beat *2 eggs* with *1 teaspoon sugar* and the leftover milk. Season with a little *salt* and pour very gently over the meat mixture (It helps to pour the custard mixture over the back of a spoon.)

Bake in a moderately hot oven (about 200°C) for an hour.

Serve hot with rice, or cold in slices.

Note: The South Africans make their rice yellow by adding turmeric to the cooking water. They also add raisins to the rice while it is cooking, and add apricot jam to the curry for a sweet–sour flavour.

'When the guests have been helped to wine and the servants have left the room the host should pass the decanters to his guests, commencing with the gentleman nearest him. The passing of the decanter is principally for the gentlemen. No lady helps herself to wine, nor has a second glass.'

CWA Coronation Cookery Book, 1937

'Dresses with long trains, worn in the street and at public places, have long been a nuisance. The *Presse* of Vienna says that a new secret society has been established in that town for the purpose of suppressing the long trains now worn by the Viennese ladies, which, according to the circular issued by the society, "are not only an obstruction to street traffic, but also, by raising enormous clouds of dust, cause considerable danger to the lungs and eyes".'

The Ladies' Treasury, 1868

EMBASSY OF SPAIN

ZARZUELA DE MARISCOS
(Seafood Casserole)

Spanish cooks use halibut for this, and Australian alternatives are schnapper, gemfish or any reef fish.

Shell *500 g (1 lb) large fresh prawns,* leaving the tails on.

Cut *500 g (1 lb) schnapper, gemfish or any reef fish* into chunks and saute the pieces in *3 tablespoons heated Spanish olive oil* in a pan. When golden, add the prawns and cook a minute or so until lightly coloured.

Add *2 tablespoons brandy* and set a match to it. When the flame dies add:

1 medium onion, chopped
1 whole garlic clove
1 pimento, diced (bottled variety will do fine)
2 tomatoes, peeled and chopped

Cook gently until very soft, then remove the garlic.

Add:

¼ cup blanched almonds, ground
1 teaspoon salt

Cook briefly then add:

½ cup white wine
10 mussels in the shell

Simmer until the mussels open.

Meanwhile, mash the garlic clove with *1 tablespoon minced parsley* and return to the sauce.

Serves 4–6.

TURKISH EMBASSY

IMAM BAYILDI

Reportedly this dish takes its name after a priest.

Cut the stems off *8 long eggplants* and peel strips of skin so they have a striped effect.

Cut a deep slit on one side of each, put them in salted water and leave for 20 minutes. Drain and dry.

In a pan with *¼ cup oil*, fry *3 medium onions*, halved and sliced. When soft add *3 garlic cloves*, finely chopped, and cook a few minutes more.

Put into a bowl with:
1 cup chopped tomatoes
¼ cup chopped parsley
salt and *pepper* to taste

Add another *¼ cup oil* to the frying pan, heat it and quickly brown the eggplants, turning all the time to brown evenly.

Leaving them in the pan, fill the slits in the eggplants with the onion mixture and spread remaining mixture on top. Pour over the juice of *one lemon* and a little *water*.

Cover the pan and simmer for 35–40 minutes until tender.

Serve at room temperature or chilled.

Parsley.

* E·A·T·I·N·G C·A·N·B·E·R·R·A *
S·T·Y·L·E

What is 'Canberra Style'? It's good home cooking — the style our mothers used; it's innovative cooking — experimenting with an exciting range of ingredients and different methods; it's home entertaining; and it's eating out in any of Canberra's 249 restaurants.

To cover them all would require several volumes so here you'll find succulent samples.

FIRST COURSES

SOUP

TOMATO AND CRAB SOUP

Mix in a saucepan:

450 g (16 oz) tin tomato soup
170 g (6 oz) tin crabmeat
¼ cup dry sherry
2 teaspoons curry powder
few drops tabasco
2 medium tomatoes, peeled and chopped
salt and *pepper*

Heat well and, just before serving, stir in *½ cup cream*. Sprinkle *parsley* on each serving.

Serves 6.

BAKED ONION SOUP

This magnificent soup, when served with a good crusty bread and a dinner wine, is a meal in itself.

In *3 tablespoons butter* in a heavy-based saucepan fry *500 g (1 lb) white onions*, sliced.

Sprinkle on and fry:
1 teaspoon paprika
4 dessertspoons plain flour

Allow to cool, while mixing:
1 pkt mushroom soup
2½ cups milk (breakfast cups)
2½ cups stock (can be made with cubes)
½ cup dry sherry

Add this mixture to the fried onions and cook for about 10 minutes, adding *salt* and *pepper* during cooking.

Pour into individual ovenproof bowls and completely cover the tops with *grated cheese*.

Bake in the oven till melted and a pale golden colour (or put under a griller for about 10 minutes).

Before taking to the table add a dob of *whipped cream* and a sprinkling of *paprika*.

Serves 6–8.

'Winter is the season of Canberra's discontent.

See the public servant slumped in his Volvo, disconsolate at being passed over in the Queen's Birthday Honours: not even an Order of Australia, let alone a KBE.

It is a time when even staunch republicans would like the right of refusal.'

Alan Fitzgerald, *Sydney Morning Herald*, June 1980

ENTREES

PÂTÉ MAISON A LA NORMANDY

This superb pâté goes well with fresh crunchy rye bread and butter.

Melt *500 g (1 lb) butter* over medium heat and add:
500 g (1 lb) fresh, washed chicken livers
250 g (8 oz) diced onions

Add:
1 bayleaf
sprinkling of mixed herbs, salt and pepper
250 g (8 oz) cooking apples, peeled and chopped

Cook until the livers turn grey in colour, and then put through a mincer.

Then, mix in a good splash each of *brandy* and *port wine*, and check the seasoning before turning into small individual moulds or one big one.

Place in the fridge to set.

Serves 6.

SCALLOPS IN WHITE WINE

In a saucepan put:
200 g (6 oz) scallops
50 g (1¾ oz) sliced champignons
1/2 cup chopped shallots
1 cup white wine (moselle)

Bring to the boil, then thicken with a roux (equal parts of *butter* and *flour* allowed to cook till bubbling in a separate saucepan).

Stir well, and just before serving stir in *½ cup fresh cream* mixed with *2 lightly beaten egg yolks*. Then add *salt* and *pepper* and a dash of *moselle*.

Don't overcook the egg yolks and cream or it will curdle.

Turn into serving bowls.

Serves 2.

ALBERT HALL

Officially opened in 1928 by the then Prime Minister, Mr (later Lord) Bruce, the hall was built to give the growing population of Canberra a distinguished cultural venue. Galvanised iron sheds had previously served the purpose.

The building was named after the Albert Hall in London and also after Albert, Duke of York, who had opened Parliament.

Speaking at the opening, Mr Bruce said: 'This is a definite step towards making Canberra the centre of Australian art and literature, and of everything that will uplift the Australian people — a centre from which will radiate all those aspirations that are truly national!'

As it turned out Albert Hall did not become the centre for Australian culture. For four decades, however, it was about the only place in Canberra where a show or a ball could be held.

While Canberra was still a bush capital many international stars appeared at the hall. Famous names include Noel Coward, Richard Tauber, Eileen Joyce and Marjorie Lawrence. Dame Edna Everage was one of the last stars to appear there.

In the early years it served the needs, not only of people in Canberra, but also of people from the surrounding countryside. Country people could come into town to shop on Saturday and attend whatever function was on in the hall at night.

Probably the greatest show ever staged at Albert Hall was the opening of the Petrov Royal Commission in 1954. Albert Hall was the only building in Canberra big enough to stage the inquiry. In the early 1960s the musical play, 'The Sentimental Bloke', had its world premiere at the hall.

At about this time the popularity of dances began to wane and with the opening of the Canberra Theatre in 1965 the hall's fortunes continued to decline. For one thing, the theatre was heated! On cold nights at the Albert Hall it was not unknown for patrons to appear for a concert complete with overcoat, rug and hot-water bottle.

The hall is still used for various functions. The day I drew it there was a market in progress and people everywhere.

Albert Hall.

One of Canberra's best known and respected citizens was Patrick (Pat) Pola who for twenty-three years owned and operated Pola's draper and mercer shop in Bentham Street, Yarralumla. Affectionately dubbed 'The Mayor of Yarralumla', he sold the shop to his daughter and son-in-law, Margaret and Kevin Wilson, just two years before his death in 1978.

Pat Pola was born in 1903 in a little goldmining town near Braidwood, called Jembaicumbere (also the birthplace of famous horse trainer, Tommy Smith). His parents ran a hotel in the town, catering mainly for the many Chinese gold-diggers in the area.

While Pat was still a young boy his mother died and, soon after, his father contracted TB. Doctors advised a move to the mountains. So Pat, aged twelve, with his ailing father went to live in the hills around Captain's Flat — equipped only with elementary camping gear and rabbit traps. Pat's schooling could best be described as 'occasional' at Braidwood School.

Thus, father and son lived for seven years until the father's death.

Pat moved to Canberra where he was befriended by Professor McKenzie, then senior academic at Duntroon Military College. He was given a job in the canteen and later became canteen manager. From that position he moved to Queanbeyan where he ran a shop, and in 1933 married Eva Finlayson whose family owned and operated the Wattle Cafe at Kingston.

Soon after, he took a position at Cusacks, for whom he worked for many years during which time he opened and managed Cusacks of Manuka (since closed). Polas' at Yarralumla opened in 1953 and was demolished to make way for a restaurant in the early 1980s.

Pat Pola was a keen and generous fisherman. Whenever he had fish to spare, he rang the Governor-General's secretary (then Murray Tyrrell) and a government car would be swiftly despatched for the fish. The reward was an invitation to meet the Queen when she came to Australia in 1964. Pat and Eva Pola were presented to Her Majesty at Government House and the whole family regarded it as the fisherman's finest hour!

YABBIES MOSKA

This recipe appeared under the title 'Prawns Moska' in Len Evans' and Graeme Kerr's book *The Galloping Gourmets*. It featured king prawns and was the creation of Nick Moska at his restaurant in New Orleans.

Len Evans suggested substituting the plentiful Lake Burley Griffin yabbies.

In a frying pan heat ¼ *cup olive oil* and in it saute for 15–20 minutes:
1 *kg (2 lb) unpeeled yabbie tails*
pinch fresh oregano
pinch fresh rosemary
pinch coarse black pepper
3 *bayleaves*
6 *garlic cloves* (finely chopped)
pinch salt

Add ¼ *cup dry white wine* and cook for another 10 minutes until the wine is nearly reduced.

Place the yabbies on a serving dish and pour the aromatic sauce over.

Serves 4.

'The first impression of Canberra is universal. Where are the people? There are automobiles drifting around the place on excellent roads. But in Canberra there are 6782 kilometres of footpaths in the entire area, and only 11 people using them at any one time.'

Max Harris, *Bulletin*, 17 June 1980

MAIN COURSES

FISH

SOLE AND SHRIMP EN PAPILOTTE (IN PAPER)

This makes an excellent luncheon dish.

For 1 person allow *1 whole sole* (with the dark skin removed).

In a skillet with a little oil and butter saute:

1 small peeled and diced tomato

1½ chopped spring onions

salt to taste

Set aside, then cut a piece of unwaxed greaseproof paper into a heart shape large enough to hold the sole on one half, and butter it.

Next, heat a large frypan and in a little *butter* and *oil* cook the sole, lightly floured, until almost cooked (about 3 minutes each side).

Put the sole onto the buttered paper, top with:

the tomato/spring onions mixture

3 medium-sized fresh cooked king prawns (shelled and deveined, of course!)

1½ chopped spring onions

Fold the paper over and seal the edges with *egg white*.

Put on a buttered baking dish and cook in a moderate to hot oven (190°C) for 15 minutes.

SCALLOPS AND LYCHEES EN BROCHETTE

Simply alternate on long skewers — one per person (or two smaller skewers) — *fresh scallops* and *tinned, drained lychees*. Sit them on a grilling rack and grill a few minutes each side, just long enough to cook the scallops.

Serve on a bed of rice if you like.

'The price of posting a letter was increased from 1½d to 2d as part of the Budget effort to reduce a deficit of £14 million.'

Canberra Times, 10 July 1930

GRILLED SCHNAPPER WITH PEACHES

For this you'll need *4 fish steaks*, cut about 2.5 cm (1 inch) thick, and *2 fresh peaches*, peeled, stoned and halved.

Blend:

2 tablespoons olive oil
½ teaspoon salt
½ teaspoon paprika
freshly ground black pepper
2 finely chopped shallots
1 teaspoon minced fresh, or ¼ teaspoon dried, thyme

Brush the fish with this seasoned oil and let stand about 15 minutes.

Arrange fish on a greased foil-lined grilling tray with peach halves on either side of the fish.

Grill the fish until it is lightly browned and flakes easily, basting both fish and peaches with *¼ cup rose wine or white wine.*

Serve with buttered noodles or rice.

Serves 4.

CURRIED FISH SUPREME

Pour hot water over *500 g (1 lb) smoked cod fillet* and soak for 10 minutes. Remove and place in warm water to cover and bring to the boil. Simmer gently for 15 minutes.

Drain and flake the fish and add to this sauce:

Melt *3 tablespoons butter* in a saucepan and stir in:

3 tablespoons plain flour
½ teaspoon salt
pinch cayenne pepper
½ level tablespoon curry powder

Cook 2 or 3 minutes, then remove from the heat to stir in *2 cups milk.* Heat, stirring all the time, until it boils and thickens.

Add:

1 tablespoon lemon juice
2 chopped or sliced hard-boiled eggs
2 level tablespoons chopped green pepper
2 level tablespoons chopped onion and parsley, mixed

Heat thoroughly and serve.

Serves 4.

TROUT McKAY

This recipe comes from a dedicated trout fisherman who says: 'Happily I usually catch enough to allow me to experiment with their cooking — this recipe is one of my favourites, and furthermore is one that I devised myself!'

Clean the *trout* in the normal manner, leaving the head and tail on for appearance's sake if desired.

Sprinkle *salt* and *pepper* in the stomach cavity, fill with *mint* (unchopped) and a *knob of butter*.

Wrap each fish firmly in lightly buttered foil and bake on a tray in an oven (or in a frypan) at 180°–190°C.

A fish of 1 kg (2 lb) will take about 20 minutes, smaller fish less, but never cook them for less than 10 minutes.

The fish may be served either hot or cold.

The flavour is improved if the fish can be left wrapped in the foil for several hours before cooking.

One of Canberra's first cafes was the Wattle Cafe at Kingston, owned and operated by the Finlayson family. It was situated in Kennedy Street near where Sylvia Parson's shop now stands.

The cafe began operating on the same day as Parliament House was opened in 1927. It served snacks and meals — often until late at night — for the early residents and visitors to Canberra. It stayed open until 2.00 am and operated every day of the week.

The cafe specialised in home cooking and was noted for its pies. Breakfasts were served, mainly to the residents of the Printers Quarters (near where Fraser Court units now stand). It was also patronised by the after-theatre crowds from the Capitol Theatre, Manuka (demolished in 1980).

POULTRY

JUNE'S CHICKEN

Use *6 chicken pieces, flour* lightly and brown them in heated *oil* in a pan. Pour off oil and transfer chicken to a casserole dish.

In the same pan put *1 dessertspoon butter* and in it saute:
2 medium onions, chopped
1 eggplant, sliced
8 shallots, chopped
2 button squash, chopped
1 green pepper, chopped
2 cloves garlic, finely chopped
Add *3 sliced tomatoes* (medium).

Cook 3 minutes and add:
1 cup stock (can be made with a cube)
½ cup red wine
1 teaspoon curry
salt and *pepper* to taste
Pour over the chicken in the casserole and bake in a moderate oven (180°C) 1–1½ hours.

CHICKEN VOGUE

For this use *4 whole chicken breasts,* skinned, *or 1 chicken* cut into serving pieces.
Add:
1 cup dry white wine
1 teaspoon salt
pepper
Bake uncovered about 20 minutes, and just before serving, stir into the pan juices:
2 egg yolks mixed with a little cream
Garnish with *sliced fresh mushrooms* which have been sauteed in butter for 5 minutes, and *tiny onions* previously cooked in *butter* and a little *water.*
Serves 4.
Note: The dish can be made without the egg yolk and cream sauce. It still tastes delicious and is better for weight watchers.

CHICKEN MORRISON

Margaret Morrison and her husband Major-General A. L. Morrison were first posted to Duntroon in 1956 when Canberra was a very small township. When asked her impressions of Canberra, Mrs Morrison said: 'I love it — I know of no other city in the world where I can spend the morning at home, lunch on the opposite side of the city, play golf in another area, visit someone on the way home, and still be home in time to prepare dinner.'

Steam *2 chickens, or 2 kg (4 lb) chicken pieces* with:
1 cup water
juice of 1 medium lemon
juice of 1 medium orange
1 onion, sliced
2 sticks celery, chopped
2 fine slices of green ginger
sprinkle each of *parsley* and *tarragon*

When the chicken is cooked and the flesh falls easily from the bone, let it cool then pull the chickens apart and dice.

Mix the diced chicken with this butter sauce:
In a saucepan melt *2 tablespoons butter.* Off the heat mix in *2 tablespoons flour* (using a wooden spoon). Cook a minute or so, and off the heat stir in gradually *300 ml (½ pint) milk* and *300 ml (½ pint) chicken stock.* Add a dash of *sherry.*

In a pan with a little butter, fry:
1 medium onion, chopped
250 g (8 oz) mushrooms, sliced
When the onion starts to brown add:
4 shallots
1 dessertspoon chopped parsley

Add all this to the chicken/butter sauce mixture and put into a casserole, top with *breadcrumbs* which have been mixed with *melted butter* and *parsley* (the amount required will depend on the size of your casserole dish).

Top the lot with *grated cheese.*

Heat through in a moderately hot oven (200°C) until it browns and bubbles. Serve with rice.

Serves 8–10.

Note: Instead of making into a casserole, the chicken mixture may be used as a filling for savoury pancakes.

CANARD AUX CERISES
(Duck with Cherries)

Place *a duckling* in a baking dish — first removing the neck and the liver.

Season it with *salt* and *pepper* and baste with *oil*.

Cook in a moderate oven (180°C). Test if it's cooked by pricking a leg — if the liquid comes clear, then it's ready.

Fillet the duckling, removing the breast and legs in one piece.

Serve with Cherry Sauce:

Put about ½ *cup pitted tinned cherries* in a saucepan with:

½ *cup juice*

½ *cup cherry brandy*

Boil until reduced by half, then sweeten to taste.

Add *demi glace* and boil again to reduce the liquid. Thicken if desired with a little *cornflour/water paste*, stirring all the time.

Pour over the duckling and serve hot.

Serves 1.

'More than justice is served in the new High Court building.

Its public canteen serves steak Diane for $3.30, fish for $2.25, and fine wines without horrendous mark-ups.

Sandwiches, sausages and pies with sauce are served, too, but it is still not the same as your average cafe.

You eat beneath a timber-panelled roof, looking through a glass wall on to the lake, lean your elbows on varnished wooden tables, snuggle into Fritz Hansen Danish look-like-fibre-glass chairs and butt cigarettes in "Trend" ashtrays made in Los Angeles.

There are trees, that look like birches, springing out of white tubs and photographs of Australian country court-houses lining the walls — sort of arty-looking, borrowed from the establishment which is to move in next door.

It will appeal to the aesthete, and to the person who works in the canteenless Trade Building nearby, to the court reporter and others.'

Rowena Stretton, *Canberra Times*, 22 July 1980

HIGH COURT OF AUSTRALIA

The new High Court of Australia was opened by Queen Elizabeth II on 26 May 1980. Constructed of concrete and glass at a cost of more than $49 million, it stands on the shores of Lake Burley Griffin.

A competition was held to select a design for the new building. It attracted 158 entries. The winner was a design by Christopher Kringas, an architect with the firm of Edwards Madigan Torzillo and Briggs Pty Ltd. Sadly he died of cancer in 1975 at the age of thirty-eight, and a commemorative slab has been set into the floor of the Public Hall.

This Public Hall is the most spectacular area in the building, with enormous glass walls at opposite ends. The whole area gives a feeling of space — in fact it contains the largest architectural space of any building in Australia.

One of the best known judges of the design competition for the building was Sir Garfield Barwick who, from the time he became Chief Justice in 1964, lobbied hard for the High Court to be permanently based in Canberra. Although the High Court had been established in 1903, it had no permanent home until 1923, when a building was constructed for it in Sydney. In 1928 another building was constructed for it in Melbourne.

The Canberra building is ten levels high. To soften the harsh effect of the concrete, carpets are in shades of rust, reds and burgundy, and timber panelling is used extensively. In order to avoid an intimidating 'peering-down' effect, the Justices' benches in the Ceremonial Courtroom are only two steps higher than the rest of the court. Sir Garfield is reported to have said: 'I have always been against having the courts raised too high.'

MRS SINGH'S CHICKEN CURRY

Several years ago in Canberra the wife of Colonel Singh, an Indian diplomat, gave Indian curry cooking lessons in her home. All who've tasted this recipe have become curry converts!

Cut a *1 kg (2 lb) chicken into small pieces* (bones and all).

Grate finely (or mash in a blender):
3 onions
2 cloves garlic
5 cm (2 inch) piece of ginger

Into a large saucepan or cast-iron casserole on a very hot stove put *½ cup cooking oil.*

When the oil is very hot (almost bubbling) add the onion, garlic and ginger. Add *1 dessertspoon salt* and stir well.

When the grated mixture starts to brown, add:
1 heaped teaspoon turmeric
1 level teaspoon chilli powder
1 heaped teaspoon coriander powder

When mixed and very hot, add the chicken pieces and mix well.

Put the lid on the saucepan or casserole dish and turn the heat down two-thirds.

After about 5 minutes add:
1 grated tomato (or a mashed, tinned tomato)
2 dessertspoons tomato paste
Stir and cover again.

After another 5 minutes add *1 cup of water* and stir well. When the mixture starts to boil, recover and let it simmer gently, stirring occasionally.

When the chicken starts to come away from the bone and a fork penetrates the flesh easily (the oil should have separated into little rivers) take the pan off the heat and let it stand for 5–10 minutes.

With a small spoon remove as much oil as you can from the top.

Reheat if necessary and serve with boiled rice.

Serves 4–6.

MEAT

BAKED LAMB SIVERTSEN

This is a different and very tasty way of baking a leg of lamb.

Rub the *leg of lamb* with *salt* and *pepper* and sprinkle lightly with *flour*.

Start baking the leg in very little fat, at 200°C, then after 15 minutes turn heat down to 150°C, and at the same time baste the meat with this mixture:

½ cup chicken stock (made with a cube)
½ cup white wine
1½ dessertspoons chopped mint
½ small onion, grated
1 clove garlic, crushed

Baste the joint with this every 15 minutes until it's cooked to the desired degree. If the mixture is all used before the joint is cooked, continue basting with the juices in the baking dish.

The flavour penetrates the whole joint and makes delicious cold meat, too.

MUM'S LAMB WITH ORANGE

Cut *750 g (1½ lb) lamb or mutton* into cubes and place in a saucepan with *water* to cover the meat, and *salt* and *pepper* to taste. Put the lid on and simmer gently 1–1½ hours or till tender.

Add:

2 slices green ginger, finely chopped
1 clove garlic, finely chopped (or *1 small onion*)
grated rind of 1 orange
2 dessertspoons soy sauce

Simmer 30 minutes more, stirring now and then, and before serving thicken with *2 dessertspoons cornflour* mixed to a paste with a little cold *water*. Keep stirring until the lot boils again.

Serves 4.

COUNTRY STYLE HOT POT

Use 2 kg (4 lb) forequarter lamb chops, trim the fat off and cut them up if you think they're a bit large.

Cut the rind off 250 g (8 oz) streaky bacon and cut into strips.

Slice:
750 g (1½ lb) carrots
750 g (1½ lb) onions

Dice:
250 g (8 oz) swede turnips

Halve:
1 kg (2 lb) potatoes (peeled)

Now put all these goodies in layers in a large casserole, topping with potatoes.

Over the lot pour a mixture of:
2½ cups tomato juice
½ teaspoon thyme, marjoram or mixed herbs
salt and pepper (about 2 teaspoons salt and good pepper shaking)
1 cup water

Dot the potatoes with butter pieces. Put the lid on (or seal with foil) and bake in a moderate oven (180°C) for 2½ - 3 hours.

Cook uncovered for the last half hour or so to brown the potatoes.

Serves 6–8.

VEAL PARISIENNE

This is very quick and easy — ideal for busy people.

You'll need 2 separate frying pans.

With a little butter and oil in one pan fry 500 g (1 lb) champignons (about 10 minutes).

In the other pan with a little butter and oil fry 4 veal steaks with 2 cloves garlic, crushed or finely chopped, and pepper and salt to taste.

When the meat is almost tender (after about 7 minutes) add a slurp of cognac and ½ cup cream.

Stir until the pan juices have made a sauce, then add the champignons.

Serve with boiled baby potatoes and vegetables or salad.

Serves 4.

BROCHETTE DE BOEUF ORIENTAL
(Skewered Beef)

Cut *500 g (1 lb) fillet steak* into cubes, thread on skewers (use 4 small or 2 longer ones) and marinate at least 12 hours in this mixture:

½ cup red wine
½ cup olive oil
pinch of salt
1 teaspoon cracked black pepper (don't use white, it leaves an odour)
½ garlic clove, crushed or very finely chopped using a knife with a little salt on the blade
1 pinch each of sage, rosemary and thyme
1 dessertspoon chopped parsley

Cover the bowl or dish with cling wrap (never silver foil because the meat will absorb the tinny flavour).

Cook on a greased hotplate, a few minutes on each side, and serve on a bed of rice flavoured with shallots, butter and white wine.

For *2 cups cooked rice* allow:
2 chopped shallots
2 teaspoons butter
1 tablespoon white wine
Serves 2.

Note: It's important to skewer the cubed meat before marinating otherwise it will become too soft to handle easily.

'Twentieth century ghetto housing. Third generation public servants with no knowledge of the real world but yet masters of it.'
Rupert Murdoch,
from a speech to the National Press Club, 1980

THE CARILLON

The Canberra Carillon, which is one of the largest in the world, was a gift from the British Government to Australia to mark Canberra's jubilee. It took seven years to complete, and in April 1970 was accepted by Queen Elizabeth on behalf of the Australian people.

The three-column tower, built by the British Ministry of Buildings and Public Works, contains the following inscription: 'Presented by Britain to the City of Canberra in commemoration of the Golden Jubilee of the founding of the National Capital of Australia — March twelve, Nineteen sixty-three.'

A carillon is an instrument containing at least two full octaves of cup-shaped bells. These are tuned, one with the other, to at least four overtones so that variations of bells played together will produce a harmonious sound. It is played by one person who sits at the keyboard, controlling the expression by the power applied to the hand batons and foot pedals. Pressure on a baton or pedal is transmitted by steel wire to a soft iron bell hammer.

The design for the Carillon was chosen from six entries in a limited design competition. The Australian and British Institutes of Architects each nominated three architects and the winner was the Australian firm of Cameron, Chisholm and Nichol.

One of the largest carillons in the world, it has fifty-three bells, the largest weighing more than six tonnes and the smallest only seven kilograms. The bells, playing keyboard and frame were made by John Taylor and Sons of England.

An interesting aspect of the Carillon is that all its wood came from one century-old oak beam which was removed from the original Taylor's factory. The use of this highly seasoned single beam accounts for the uniform texture and beauty of all the wood in the instrument.

Situated on Aspen Island in Lake Burley Griffin, the Carillon is a favoured place for wedding ceremonies, and regular Sunday recitals provide immense pleasure for those lucky enough to be in the vicinity.

The Carillion — A.C.T.

During the 1940s and 1950s the old Acton Guest House was home to many public servants and the venue for many a party.

One evening a practical joke was played on a fellow who was out until the early hours of the morning.

Residents removed the light bulbs from his room and, due to the close proximity of a horse paddock, managed to smuggle one of the animals into the room.

Imagine the poor fellow's consternation when he returned home, pressed the light switches and in total blackness found himself on a collision course with a horse!

SWISS BLISS

This is great on a freezing Canberra evening when the winds are howling and the rain is drizzling outside.

Spread a baking tray with aluminium foil and rub *15 g (½ oz) butter* over it.

Cut *1 kg (2 lb) blade or round steak* into 2.5 cm (1 inch) thick serving portions, and arrange on the foil, overlapping each piece.

Sprinkle with :
1 pkt French Onion soup
½ green pepper, chopped
2 medium tomatoes, sliced

Season with *salt* and *pepper*.

Pour over a mixture of:
1 tablespoon Worcestershire sauce
1 cup tomato juice
1 tablespoon cornflour

Cover the lot with another sheet of foil, seal the edges and stand the parcel in a baking dish and cook in a moderate oven (180°C) for 2 hours.

Sprinkle with *parsley* just before serving.
Serves 4.

MY MOTHER-IN-LAW'S WAY WITH PORK

Anne Loveridge, army wife and journalist, says:

'When Rosemary asked me for a recipe I was flattered and frightened. Flattered that she thought me a good enough cook, frightened because I am a fearful cook. Fear in the fright sense, for as much as I like being invited out to dinner I always leave with a sense of shame. Shame that my culinary efforts could never match those of the dinner which we have just had. Everyone else's food always seems to taste so much better. Perhaps not having had to sweat and slave over a hot stove has a lot to do with it. Going through my recipe book was a trip down memory lane: jam and preserves made when we had a hedge of blackberries in England; curries and exotic dishes collected during two years in Bangkok; magnificent fruit puddings using the tropical fruits we had growing round our house in Papua New Guinea. But what I really wanted for you was a typical Australian recipe. I could find none; all I can come up with are a few hints and suggestions gathered during thirty plus years of cooking. Here is one — a delicious way of cooking pork.'

First, slit the skin well into the fat then coat with a liberal amount of fresh lemon juice and place under the griller for a few minutes. When roasting in the normal way, add more lemon juice. It not only makes the best crackling in the world, but also the lemon flavour seeps in.

By a Woman
'It should be observed that seemingly political actions which proceed from the heart, as most certainly they would do if women had the franchise, are not politics, and that in all ages the interference of women in the legislature has proved either ridiculous, useless, or fatal.'

The Ladies' Treasury, 1868

HOTEL CANBERRA

Following a Cabinet decision to arrange accommodation for Parliamentarians and visitors to the city, building of the hotel was begun in 1922. It was completed and opened in 1924. By 1927, when Parliament moved to the national capital, it had already become a popular meeting place for politicians, journalists and public servants.

The architect was John Smith Murdoch. The ciphers for the silver, crockery and linen were all designed by the architect's office and the furniture and furnishings were made specially for the hotel.

A Canberra journal of 1927 described the Hotel Canberra as:

undoubtedly the next most important building in the city (after Parliament House) from the point of view of cost, which was in the vicinity of £140,000. It boasts equipment, service, comfort, and appearance equal to that of modern city hotels, with the additional benefit of not being cramped. The building is the shape of a starfish. This gives a maximum of light and air. Within the central portions are

Hotel Canberra.

grassed courtyards and gardens, while surrounding the pavilions, and for some distance around the whole structure, are beautiful lawns and gardens — truly an oasis in a desert of fresh-turned earth, and new laid brickwork. It too has a white exterior, with red-tiled roof.

The hotel, which could accommodate nearly 200 guests, had lounges, sitting rooms, card and writing rooms, a billiard room and an extensive dining room. Adjoining the hotel were tennis courts, a bowling green and croquet greens (the latter still in use), as well as a nine-hole golf course. The tariff was £1 2s 6d per day or seven pounds a week. From 1924 to 1928 the hotel was 'dry' because of general prohibition: everybody had to go across the border to Queanbeyan.

In 1974 the hotel became a government office building, and operated as such for several years.

At the time of writing a redevelopment plan is underway, so that this beautiful landmark will once again operate as a prestige hotel. The emphasis will be on preserving its old-style character while providing quality accommodation of the highest international standard.

GRAMRODE FRIKADELLER

Mince:
750 g (1½ lb) lean pork
750 g (1½ lb) beef

Mix together:
the meat
2 large onions, chopped

Add:
salt
pinch sugar
¼ teaspoon ground cloves
1 litre (1¾ pints) milk
1 teacup self-raising flour
3 eggs

Mix to a fairly firm consistency. Take dessertspoons of the mixture and fry in hot oil on medium heat until golden brown. Turn and fry the other side. (2 minutes each side should be sufficient.)

These go very well with red cabbage and mashed potatoes.

Makes about 100.

Note: Frikadeller is usually made with just pepper and salt, but the ground cloves give a specially nice flavour.

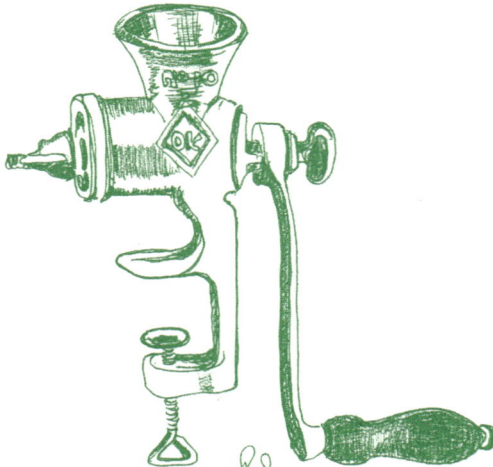

- mincer -

VEAL AND MUSHROOMS

Have ready *750 g (1½ lb) veal pieces* coated with a mixture of:
2 level tablespoons plain flour
1½ teaspoons salt
½ teaspoon pepper
Heat *2 tablespoons butter* in a pan, brown the veal with *1 large sliced onion* and *2 cloves garlic*, finely chopped.
Transfer the lot to another dish and into the pan put:
1 large tin (440 g or 16 oz) tomato puree
¾ cup stock (can be made from a beef or chicken cube)
2 level tablespoons brown sugar
Simmer about 5 minutes and return veal mixture to the pan.
Cover and cook slowly (on top of stove or in the oven at 115°C).
Just before serving add *125 g (4 oz) fresh mushrooms* sauteed in a little butter (or use tinned champignons) and lastly stir in *⅓ cup dry or medium sherry*.
Serve with rice, or noodles sprinkled with poppy seeds.
Serves 4–6.

HAM AND TOMATO NOODLES

Cook *250 g (8 oz) noodles* in boiling salted water until tender (about 20 minutes). Drain and set aside.
Saute in a little butter in a pan:
175 g (6 oz) rindless bacon rashers, chopped
1 large onion, chopped
salt and *pepper* to taste
1 teaspoon oregano
Add:
425 g (15 oz) tin tomatoes, undrained and slightly mashed
1 tablespoon chopped chives or parsley (or both)
Stir and simmer a few minutes. Remove from the heat and mix with the noodles. Put the mixture in a shallow ovenproof dish, top with a layer of *2 cups grated tasty cheese*, then *2 cups breadcrumbs* mixed with *250 g (8 oz) butter*, melted.
Bake in a hot oven for about 20–25 minutes.
Serve with French salad and garlic bread.
Serves 4–6.

MEATLESS DISHES

STUFFED EGGPLANT

Cut *3 medium eggplants* in half lengthwise, sprinkle with *1 tablespoon salt* and lie face down on a clean tea towel for 30 minutes to extract as much water from them as possible.

Place them in a shallow roasting dish and pour *2 tablespoons of olive oil* over them. Put under a hot grill for 10–15 minutes until tender and slightly browned.

Remove the flesh from the eggplants, chop it and place in a mixing bowl.

Next, cook in *1 tablespoon olive oil, 250 g (8 oz) finely chopped onion* until tender and add to the eggplant.

Chop finely *500 g (1 lb) mushrooms* and twist them in a cloth to extract moisture. Cook these in *1 level tablespoon butter* and *1 tablespoon olive oil* until lightly browned. Add to the eggplant mixture.

Next, add:
150 g (5 oz) cream cheese, beaten smooth
4 tablespoons chopped parsley
½ teaspoon basil, or ¼ teaspoon thyme
Salt and *pepper* to taste
Preheat the oven to 200°C.
Fill the eggplant shells with the mixture and top with a mixture of:
3 tablespoons grated Swiss cheese
3 tablespoon dry white breadcrumbs
Baste with *melted butter.*

Put the stuffed eggplant in a baking dish with about 3 mm (1/8 inch) water and bake for 25–35 minutes until the topping browns and the mixture is thoroughly heated through.
Serves 6.

'If you eat you're involved in agriculture.'

Primary Industry Slogan

PASTA WITH CREAM CHEESE AND WALNUTS

First, boil *250 g (8 oz) pasta shells* in salted water until tender (about 20 minutes). Drain.

Now prepare the sauce.

In a fireproof serving dish melt:

125 g (4 oz) butter
180 g (6 oz) cream cheese

Heat gently — don't boil.

Into this mixture put the drained pasta and mix well, then add:

4 tablespoons grated parmesan cheese
60 g (2 oz) roughly chopped walnuts

Serves 6.

ZUCCHINI QUICHE

Cheddar Cheese Pastry
Sift into a bowl:

1½ cups plain flour
¼ teaspoon salt
½ teaspoon baking powder

Rub in *125 g (4 oz) butter*, add *125 g (4 oz) grated cheese* and mix to a soft dough with *milk*. Roll out between greaseproof paper and line a pie plate or quiche tray.

Filling
Saute *500 g (1 lb) zucchinis*, sliced, in *60 g (2 oz) butter* in a covered saucepan for about 3 minutes (the zucchini should be still crisp).

Beat *2 eggs* with *¼ teaspoon cream of tartar* and fold in:

½ teaspoon garlic powder
½ teaspoon salt
1 tablespoon plain flour
1½ cups light sour cream

Now, arrange the zucchini in the pastry case and cover with the egg and cream mixture.

Top with *125 g (4 oz) grated cheese* and *soft breadcrumbs* and bake in a moderate oven (190°C) for 30–35 minutes.

Serve very hot.

Serves 6–8.

CHAKCHOUKA

This dish, a variation on ratatouille, is very colourful and needs only hot buttered toast as an accompaniment for a lunch or supper dish.

Place in a pan:

250 g (8 oz) onions, sliced
500 g (1 lb) eggplant, cut into walnut-sized pieces
500 g (1 lb) green capsicum, seeded and sliced
500 g (1 lb) tomatoes, skinned and roughly chopped

Sprinkle generously with freshly ground *black pepper*, a little *salt* and pour over *1 cup olive oil*.

Simmer very gently with the lid on, for about 30 minutes. Then remove the lid and continue cooking until it evaporates and thickens.

Transfer to a greased baking dish and spread evenly, crushing any large lumps.

Make indentations with the back of a spoon, spaced evenly apart, to take *6 eggs*. Do not allow the egg whites to spread over the top of the mixture.

Sprinkle on the eggs a mixture of *½ teaspoon salt* and *½ teaspoon mild paprika*.

Cook in a moderate oven (180°C) until the whites are set. Decorate with black olives.

Serves 6.

GREEN BEAN BAKE

Cook *500 g (1 lb) beans* cut into short pieces in a little *salted water*, then saute in *¼ cup butter* for a minute.

Mix together:

1½ cups white sauce
3 lightly beaten eggs
3 tablespoons grated sharp cheese
pinch of nutmeg
the beans

Transfer to a 6-cup buttered soufflé dish and bake in a moderate oven (180°C) for 45 minutes.

Cool for 15 minutes before serving.

Serves 4.

DANISH RED CABBAGE

Shred finely:
1 *medium cabbage*
1 *green apple*, peeled
In a heavy saucepan melt 2 *tablespoons butter* and add 2 *tablespoons sugar.*
Add:
the cabbage and apple
2 *tablespoons vinegar*
½ *tablespoon salt*
*½ *to 1 cup water*
Simmer until cooked (about 15 minutes), stirring occasionally, and just before serving, stir in about ½ *cup of red currant jam or jelly.*
*If the cabbage is fresh, use less water; if it is dry, use more water.

ORANGE SWEET POTATO

Boil 1 *large sweet potato*, peeled and chopped. Drain and mash with 1 *good tablespoon butter, salt* and *pepper.*
Add:
½ *cup orange juice*
½ *teaspoon orange rind*
Turn into a casserole dish, sprinkle with *brown sugar* and ½ *teaspoon cinnamon*, and dot with *butter.*
Put in fairly slow oven (150°C) until the brown sugar melts.
Serves 6.

'A Sydney businessman, Mr F. H. Stewart, complained that he had received no reply to his offer to convert The Lodge, in which the Prime Minister, Mr Scullin, had decided not to live, into a refuge for poor women.'

Canberra Times, 9 July 1920

NATIONAL LIBRARY OF AUSTRALIA

This building, recognised as one of Canberra's most attractive, was erected by the National Capital Development Commission. Work began in 1964 and the library was opened in 1968. It is five storeys high and stands on a spacious podium in which there are two basement floors.

Only the finest materials were used in the building: Norwegian slate for the podium paving, South Australian black granite for the handrails, and white Italian marble for the forty-four columns surrounding the building. It has bronze window frames and the roof is sheathed in copper. The foyer is paved with golden Australian Wondeyan marble, the foyer staircase is of Pentelic marble from the Parthenon Quarry in Greece, and the stairwell is of blue-green Italian marble.

All the furniture and most of the soft furnishings were designed and made in Australia. For the internal finishing of the building, many Australian timbers were used, including jarrah, red cedar and Tasmanian oak.

The lower ground floor provides public facilities such as a readers' lounge, cafeteria and conference room. There are exhibition areas and a theatre which seats 300 people. Free showings of films drawn from the library collections are regularly offered to the public, particularly during school holidays.

Three tapestries in the foyer were designed by a French artist and woven in Australia. Each is five metres high and three metres wide. Australian artist Leonard French designed and executed sixteen windows which flank the exhibition areas. Each is over three metres high and a metre wide.

The library holds many precious items, probably the most valued being Captain Cook's handwritten journal of the voyage of the *Endeavour* between 1768 and 1771. The collections include material in many languages and from many countries. There is a great collection of Australian books and manuscripts, many of which have been acquired by gift or bequest. The library contains the manuscripts and papers of artists and writers, politicians and administrators, scientists and many others.

The main reading room seats more than 150 readers, with several other reading rooms catering for specific research needs.

DESSERTS

MARIE'S CHEESECAKE

Base

Crush *180 g (6 oz) Nice biscuits* into fine crumbs. Melt *90 g (3 oz) butter*, pour over the crumb mixture and press into a torte tin. Allow to set in the refrigerator.

Filling

Cream together:

3 pkts Philadelphia cream cheese
½ cup caster sugar

Add:

1 egg
½ teaspoon vanilla

Beat well, pour into the crumb base and bake 20 minutes in a slow oven (120°C). Then turn the oven off, leaving the cheesecake in until cool.

Refrigerate at least 2 hours (or overnight preferably).

To serve, top with sweetened whipped cream and sprinkle with nutmeg.

VIV'S CHESTNUT CREAM

Rich and delicious, this is served to conclude a light main course.

Put in a mixing bowl or blender:

1 tin chestnut puree
1½ cups fresh cream
1 tablespoon icing sugar (or to taste)
1 tablespoon hazelnuts or other crushed nuts
1 dessertspoon Tia Maria liqueur

Whip all together or blend for one second.

Chill, and before serving time transfer portions to small glass bowls or short-stemmed glasses (claret glasses would do).

Serve each topped with a swirl of *whipped cream*, a few *slivered almonds*, and a dribble of Tia Maria over all.

Serves 4.

Note: Chocolate shavings can be substituted for the crushed nuts in the chestnut mixture and on top.

MARDI'S GOLDEN PUFF DUMPLINGS

Sift into a basin:
1 cup self-raising flour
pinch of salt
Rub in:
1 dessertspoon butter
Add:
1 beaten egg
and *a little milk* if necessary to make a dry dough (use a knife for mixing).
Shape the dough into small dumplings (makes 10).
Place these ingredients into a large saucepan or casserole and heat until boiling:
1 cup water
½ cup sugar
1 dessertspoon butter
1 tablespoon golden syrup
Put in the dumplings all at once and cook gently 15–20 minutes.

BRANDIED WHITE GRAPES

Wash and remove the stems from *500 g (1 lb) seedless white grapes.*
Put them in a serving bowl and over them pour this mixture:
1 teaspoon lemon juice
¼ cup strained honey
2 tablespoons brandy
Let stand in the refrigerator overnight and before serving add a scoop of *sour cream* on top (½ cup for 4 serves).
Serves 4.

CHOCOLATE SHERRY LOG

Sandwich together *1 packet of chocolate flavoured biscuits*, with *whipped cream* and *raspberry jam*.
Sprinkle liberally with *sherry* and allow to stand for at least 24 hours.
A couple of hours prior to serving, coat thickly with well-beaten *cream*, and top with *grated milk chocolate*.
Serves 6.

PARLIAMENT HOUSE

The inaugural meeting of our Commonwealth Parliament took place on 9 May 1901, and it was a right royal occasion.

When Queen Victoria died only three weeks after Australia celebrated federation, her eldest son assumed the throne as King Edward VII. His son was sent to represent the English monarch at the opening of the new dominion's first Parliament.

The event was staged in Melbourne's Exhibition Hall, the largest building in the country at the time. Melbourne was established as the temporary national capital and seat of government and held that distinction for more than a quarter of a century.

A 'temporary' Parliament House was opened in Canberra by the Duke of York (later King George V) on 9 May 1927. By the 1950s this building had become an aging and inadequate structure which was unsuited to the needs of a modern legislature in a growing nation.

The design for the new permanent Parliament House was selected from many that were entered in a design competition launched in 1979.

Capital Hill was chosen as the most appropriate site. It was recognised as the most important single site in Walter Burley Griffin's vision of the capital. He conceived of Capital Hill as the true centre of Canberra and the physical and symbolic centre of the nation. In a more irreverent vein, author Alan Fitzgerald, in his book *From Living in Canberra* (1975), noted that: 'Capital Hill is appropriate for a Parliament because it was once the haunt of the nineteenth-century bushrangers.'

An attractive feature of the Mitchell/Giurgola and Thorp design is its simple imagery. Whether viewed from ground level or from the air, the building's geometry is in line with the radiating road system.

Griffin designed wide tree-lined avenues radiating like spokes of a wheel from Capital Hill. Each avenue was named after a state capital and pointed in the geographical direction of that capital, hence Sydney, Melbourne, Hobart, Adelaide, Perth and Brisbane Avenues.

Building on the new site began in 1981 and is due to be completed in 1988 — Australia's bicentenary year.

LEMON ICE CREAM

This is very cheap and good — for up to twelve people and great for hot Canberra days.

Chill *a tin of evaporated milk*, turn it into a bowl and beat until stiff.

Grate the rind of *3 lemons* and reserve it.

Add juice of lemons and beat until even stiffer.

In a separate bowl beat the yolks of *2 eggs* and:

a small part of *1 cup sugar*
rind of the lemons

Beat the egg whites separately, and when stiff add the rest of the sugar. Beat well.

To the evaporated milk add first the yolk mixture, then the white mixture and freeze.

Topping

Mix together:

2 cups crushed cornflakes
1 large tablespoon brown sugar
2 tablespoons melted butter

Either sprinkle on top of the ice cream or turn out the ice cream and press all over like a cake.

BRANDIED CHOCOLATE MOUSSE

Separate *4 eggs*.

In a double saucepan over boiling water melt *125 g (4 oz) dark chocolate*. Cool. Mix into the well-beaten egg yolks.

Fold in:

3 cups thickly whipped cream
1 teaspoon brandy
4 egg whites, stiffly beaten

Put into a glass bowl, or individual serving dishes, and chill before serving.

Serves 6.

* S·O·M·E B·A·K·I·N·G D·A·Y *
F·A·V·O·U·R·I·T·E·S

Many of us still set aside a special day for baking goodies to fill the tummies and the tins — and make extras for the freezer, an unknown facility in the old days!

While recipes in this section are favourites with Canberra cooks, I'm sure their appeal is universal.

FIVE-MINUTE TEA CAKE

Blend well:
¼ cup butter
⅔ cup sugar
Add:
1 beaten egg, mixed with ¾ cup milk
(It'll look curdly, but don't worry!)
Then:
1½ cups self-raising flour
pinch salt
Beat for one minute, then pour into a greased 23 cm (9 inch) round tin.
Sprinkle the top with a mixture of:
½ cup mixed fruit
¼ teaspoon cinnamon
1½ teaspoons sugar
Bake in a moderate oven 30–35 minutes, split and slather with butter while warm — or just eat as it is.
Note: The topping may be changed to sliced, cored apple, cinnamon and sugar.

CHOCOLATE CAKE

This can be served as a sweet with ice cream or cream, or served with coffee.

Beat together in a mixer, on medium speed for 3–4 minutes:

2 eggs
½ cup milk
125 g (4 oz) caster sugar
180 g (6 oz) self-raising flour
3 tablespoons cocoa
125 g (4 oz) soft butter

Turn into a 18 cm (7 inch) cake tin and bake for 1 hour in a moderate oven (180°C).

When cold, slice into 3 parts. Take the middle portion, crumble it into a bowl and pour over *1 tablespoon rum or brandy.* Let soak for a while, then add:

1 cup sour cream
½ cup chopped walnuts
½ cup glace cherries

Mix well and layer it between the other two slices. Now, ice all over with chocolate icing.

Chocolate Icing
Mix to a smooth consistency:

90 g (3 oz) butter
125 g (4 oz) icing sugar
3 dessertspoons cocoa
1 dessertspoon coffee essence (or 1 teaspoon instant coffee dissolved in 1 dessertspoon hot water)
1 dessertspoon rum or brandy

Spread over the cake and decorate with *walnuts* and *cherries.*

'Mr Gabb (ALP) caused a stir in the House of Representatives by arguing that there was no need for the Parliamentary dining rooms or bar on the basis that Members could just as easily walk to their hotels. The exercise, he said, would do them good.'

Canberra Times, 24 July 1930

TESSIE'S BOILED FRUIT CAKE

In a saucepan put:
250 g (8 oz) butter
2 cups sugar
500 g (1 lb) mixed fruit
500 g (1 lb) sultanas
250 g (8 oz) raisins
125 g (4 oz) walnuts, halved
½ cup chopped dates
1½ cups water
2 level teaspoons bicarbonate of soda
Simmer over low heat (with the lid on) for 10 minutes or until the fruit swells.

Cool slightly, then add:
4 eggs, lightly beaten
2 cups plain flour, sifted with a pinch of salt
½ teaspoon mixed spice
Finally, stir in 2 tablespoons dark rum, put in a tin lined with a double thickness of greased brown paper and bake in a slow oven (120°C–135°C) for 3 to 4 hours, or until a straw or skewer inserted in the centre comes out clear.
Cool in the tin.

DATE LOAF

Pour 1 cup boiling water over 1 cup stoned dates and mash.
Combine in a bowl:
the mashed dates
1 tablespoon dripping
1 cup brown sugar
1 beaten egg
2 cups plain flour
1 teaspoon vanilla
1 teaspoon bicarbonate of soda
Mix well, turn into a greased loaf tin and bake in a moderate oven (180°C) for about 30 minutes.

*The Lodge —
Prime Minister's Residence*

THE LODGE

The Lodge was built during 1926–27 as a temporary residence for the Prime Minister. It was designed by Oakey and Parkes, a Melbourne firm of architects. The builder was Mr J. G. Taylor of Glebe, NSW, and the total cost, including development of the grounds, was £28 319.

During the course of construction it was referred to as the Prime Minister's 'house', 'cottage' or 'residence'. The first reference to it as a 'lodge' seems to be in a letter, dated 19 April 1927, from Sir John Butters, Chief Commissioner of the Federal Capital Commission, to the architects.

The Lodge was first occupied by the Prime Minister and Mrs Bruce on 4 May 1927. The initial domestic staff consisted of Miss Macdonald, who was the housekeeper, two maids and a

High walls surrounding
the lodge retain
privacy and reduce
noise level from
adjacent busy
thoroughfare!

— Rosemary Sinclair.

handyman. This latter was needed, in the words of Mrs Bruce, 'to milk the cows, bring in the wood, keep the boiler going and those sort of odd jobs'.

In 1978 the dining room, which formerly seated only twelve — or, at a pinch, fourteen — was enlarged to seat twenty-four.

In 1979, the Lodge and Government House were opened to the public for the first time and about 7000 people visited each residence. Since then it has been opened to the public on an annual basis.

Areas open to the public include: the dining room; the entrance hall, where visitors are normally received; the drawing room, with paintings on loan by the National Gallery; and the sitting room, originally designed and used as a billiard room, and now displaying other paintings on loan from the Gallery.

QUICK AND EASY PUMPKIN CAKE

This is very economical.

First mix all these ingredients:

125 g (4 oz) melted butter
1 cup cold mashed cooked pumpkin
2 tablespoons golden syrup
1 teaspooon mixed spice
2 cups sifted self-raising flour
1 pkt (250 g or 375 g) mixed fruit

Stir in:

3 eggs, beaten
¾ cup milk

(Unless making it for children, try the addition of a little rum for a specially exotic flavour.)

Bake in a greased paper-lined tin at 150°C for 3 hours.

DATE AND APRICOT CHEWS

Combine in a bowl:

1 cup chopped dates
½ cup chopped dried apricots
1 cup sugar
1 cup coconut
1 cup self-raising flour

Melt together:

125 g (4 oz) melted butter
1 dessertspoon golden syrup
1 beaten egg

Mix all together, spread into a flat dish and bake at 190°C for 20 minutes.

Cut into squares while still warm, but leave in the tin until cold.

'Canberra has a soul because I know so many people who struggled to make it a worthwhile place in which to live. When people settled in the district they had no comforts and everything had to be done the hard way — these are the people who've given the city a soul.'

Jane Southwell

GEM SCONES

Cream:
1 rounded tablespoon butter and
2 tablespoons sugar
Add:
1 egg and beat well
Stir in:
1 teacup milk, then
2 teacups sifted self-raising flour
When you begin to mix, put the gem irons in the oven to heat. When greasing them (use a brush or wad of paper) they should be hot enough to sizzle. Only half fill the cups, and cook in a brisk oven 10–12 minutes. Do not open the door for 8 or 9 minutes.
Note: 60 g (2 oz) dried fruit may be added to the mixture.
Use teacups, not large cups, and use the same cup to measure the flour and milk.

CHOCOLATE BRANDY BALLS

These are easy, delicious and look superb.
Cream:
125 g (4 oz) butter
2 cups sifted icing sugar
When light and fluffy add:
180 g (6 oz) sultanas, chopped
125 g (4 oz) glace cherries, chopped
90 g (3 oz) walnuts, chopped
Mix in *2 tablespoons brandy*, refrigerate the mixture about 30 minutes until it firms.
Roll teaspoon lots into balls and refrigerate again to firm.
Prepare this Chocolate Coating.
Melt in a saucepan:
125 g (4 oz) dark chocolate
30 g (1 oz) copha
Dip each ball into this (or skewer each ball and pour chocolate over).
Place on a tray covered with greaseproof paper and press a *walnut* on top of each. Keep refrigerated.

BEST-EVER PIKELETS

Sift together into a bowl:
1 cup self-raising flour
½ teaspoon bicarbonate of soda
¼ teaspoon salt
Add (or plop in!):
1 egg
2 tablespoons sugar
1 tablespoon butter, melted
Mix *1 teaspoon vinegar* with *1 cup milk* and mix into the other ingredients. Stir until the mixture becomes smooth and of pouring consistency.
Drop spoonfuls into a greased frypan (electric 180°C), turning as the bubbles form.

MRS GREY'S PUMPKIN SCONES

Beat to a cream:
1 tablespoon butter
½ cup sugar
Add:
1 cup salted, boiled, mashed pumpkin
1 egg
Add:
3 cups sifted self-raising flour
Turn onto a board, roll out and cut into shapes. (If too stiff, add a little *milk* before rolling out.)
Bake on a greased tray in a hot oven (230°C) for 15 minutes.

MRS McDONALD'S PLAIN SCONES

The secret of successful scones is to work fast and light — handle the dough as little as possible, use a knife for stirring, and then just plop the dough onto a lightly floured board, shape (don't knead) and cut gently in required shapes. Brush the tops with milk and get that tray into the oven as fast as possible!

Sift into a bowl:

4 cups self-raising flour with a pinch of cream of tartar added
1 teaspoon salt

Add:

1 teaspoon caster sugar

Mix in with a knife:

2 cups lukewarm milk, with
2 tablespoons cream

Put onto a floured board, gently flatten a bit and cut into shapes.

Put on a greased tray, brush with milk and bake in a very hot oven until browned and cooked — about 15 minutes.

CHEESE BISCUITS

These biscuits are very easy and a great standby for unexpected visitors.

Mix in a bowl:

375 g (¾ lb) butter
500 g (1 lb) grated tasty cheese
4 cups self-raising flour
salt and cayenne pepper to taste

When well mixed, roll into balls between the palms of the hands, place on greased biscuit trays and press flat with a fork.

Cook at 150°C until light brown (about 20 minutes).

* I·N·D·E·X O·F R·E·C·I·P·E·S *
(and recipe contributors)